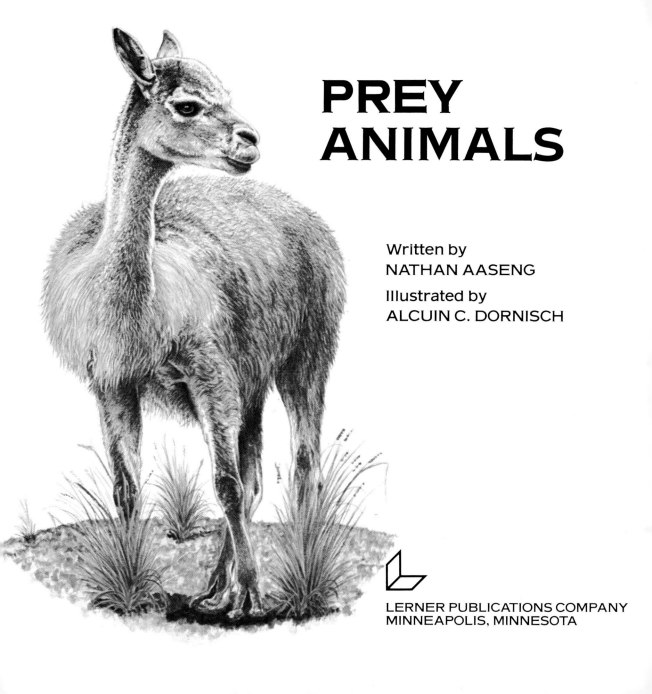

PREY ANIMALS

Written by
NATHAN AASENG

Illustrated by
ALCUIN C. DORNISCH

LERNER PUBLICATIONS COMPANY
MINNEAPOLIS, MINNESOTA

A NOTE ABOUT THE MEASUREMENTS IN THIS BOOK

Height is the animal's height while standing. *Length* is the length of the animal's head and body. In comparison to the animals on page 48, the boy is 4 feet (120 cm) and the woman is 5½ feet (165 cm) tall.

To Evan

AN EARLY NATURE PICTURE BOOK

Copyright © 1987 by Lerner Publications Company
All rights reserved. International copyright secured. No part of this book may be reproduced in any form whatsoever without permission in writing from the publisher except for the inclusion of brief quotations in an acknowledged review.

Library of Congress Cataloging-in-Publication Data

Aaseng, Nathan.
  Prey animals.

  (An Early nature picture book)
  Summary: Describes ten plant-eating animals who serve as food for predators, such as zebras and jackrabbits.
  1. Predation (Biology)—Juvenile literature. 2. Herbivores—Juvenile literature. 3. Animal defenses—Juvenile literature. [1. Herbivores. 2. Animals] I. Dornisch, Alcuin C., ill. II. Title. III. Series
QL758.A27   1987   599′.053   87-4036
ISBN 0-8225-1121-5 (lib. bdg.)

Manufactured in the United States of America

1 2 3 4 5 6 7 8 9 10 96 95 94 93 92 91 90 89 88 87

CONTENTS

The table of contents for this book could almost be called a menu. Included are some of the favorite foods of meat-eating animals. These "meals-on-legs" may be bite-sized dishes. Or they may be large enough to provide a feast for a **pride** of lions (a group of 15 to 20 beasts). But no matter what their size, prey animals are marked targets. They can never feel safe.

Some prey animals such as deer and antelopes enjoy some protection as they can defend themselves with sharp horns or antlers. More importantly, they have the ability to run faster than their enemies. The largest and strongest of those animals can usually **survive**, or continue to live. Only the old, the weak, or the sick are in great danger of being killed. However, any one of the animals in this book could be killed at any time by its enemies.

The creatures in this book are gentle and peaceful. They do not attack other animals. Yet they are always under attack. Although it seems that nature has left them defenseless against dangerous meat-eaters, each has been given some defense. The most obvious example is the porcupine, with its sharp quills. Others such as hares are fast runners. Zebras and tapirs will bite. Lemmings have coats that help them stay hidden. The okapi (page 5) takes cover in the thickly growing forests of Central Africa.

The fact is that none of these defenses really works well. Meat-eaters have been living off these creatures for thousands of years. Foxes and owls can spot even the smallest lemming. Not even the strongest zebra has a chance against a lion. Meat-eaters manage to catch the fastest runners and find the cleverest hiders.

It seems that nature has given the prey animals a bad deal. Yet most of these **species**, or kinds of animals, have no trouble surviving. In fact, in the game of survival, some of these "victims" have the advantage over their larger, more powerful enemies. They can get along nicely without meat-eaters, but meat-eaters can't get along without them. If meat-eaters kill too many of the prey animals, they are left without food for the future. Enough prey animals must survive to keep nature in balance.

One way that nature keeps this balance is by birthrates. Many prey animals produce babies much faster than their predators do. This means that they can recover more quickly from a disaster. Sometimes, famine will kill most of the animals in an area. Species of larger meat-eaters will take many years to recover. Prey animals, however, can often build their numbers back up more quickly. It may be a dangerous world for the prey animals. But they are able to replace themselves fast enough so that their species do not die out.

ARCTIC LEMMING

The tiny lemming does not have much of a chance for a long life. Three out of every ten of these furry, ratlike creatures die every month. Owls, foxes, ravens, and even polar bears have little trouble catching lemmings.

Even though they are threatened by so many meat-eaters, most lemmings die because there are simply too many of them. Every few years, thousands of lemmings are forced to move to a less crowded area. So many drown in oceans and lakes in these mass **migrations**, or moves, that people once thought they committed **suicide**, or killed themselves. Now we know that the lemmings are just trying to reach new homes. They are very good swimmers and do not realize that the oceans are too wide for them to swim across.

Most lemmings live on the **tundra**, the cold, treeless areas of the far north, where they feed on moss, grass, and plants. Lemmings have long, thick coats that keep them warm in winter. These coats are waterproof, so the animals can swim in cold waters without freezing.

The lemmings' only protection against meat-eaters is to stay hidden, so they shed their white fur every summer. Brown fur grows in to help them blend in with the brownish land. In the autumn, lemmings shed their brown fur for white to help them hide in the snow. During the winter, they dig tunnels under the snow's surface to find plants and berries. Arctic foxes, however, can uncover the hidden creatures. They listen for the squeaks of the lemmings beneath the snow. Then they jump high in the air and break through the crust of the snow. Weasels, too, can find their way into lemming tunnels.

Even with all of their enemies, there are more lemmings around than animals are able to eat. That is because female lemmings can give birth when they are barely a month old, and they can have as many as four **litters**, or sets, of babies in a year. With three to seven babies in each litter, there are soon so many lemmings that they practically trip over each other! Every three or four years, the area becomes so crowded that many animals must move away. Most of these die, and the remaining ones quickly build up the numbers again. And so the cycle continues.

Lemming

Length: 3-6 in. (8-15 cm)
Weight: ½-4 oz. (14-112 g)
Habitat: tundra of Asia, Europe, and North America
Food: mosses and grasses
Young: 3-7 after a pregnancy of 3 weeks
Life Span: less than 2 years in the wild

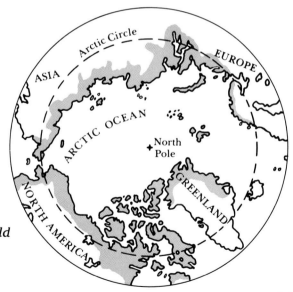

FLYING SQUIRREL

Squirrels can be found all over the world. Wherever they live, these bushy-tailed creatures are hunted. Foxes, raccoons, weasels, bobcats, owls, and hawks are a few of the animals that eat them.

Some squirrels hide while others climb trees to escape their many enemies. Flying squirrels take to the air. They do not really fly, but they can glide through the air nearly as far as the length of a football field. Many animals that eat squirrels can only catch them when they are on the ground. This gliding skill helps flying squirrels move from one tree to another without having to risk running on the ground. It also comes in handy when the squirrels are chased by climbing animals such as martens.

Before they jump, flying squirrels tilt their heads from side to side to measure the distance. Then they jump, spreading out the flaps of skin between their arms and legs.

This stretches the flaps so they act like a parachute. Flying squirrels steer by moving their tails. When they reach their target, they use the skin flaps as brakes. This slows them down so they land gently on a tree trunk.

Gliding, however, has a drawback. An animal can't stay hidden when it is flying through the air. If the squirrels did their gliding in daylight, they would attract the attention of hawks and owls. For this reason, flying squirrels stay hidden during the day. They like to make nests in hollow parts of trees. Only when it is dark will they come out to search for nuts, acorns, fruit, and insects.

Flying squirrels do not **hibernate**, or sleep, through the winter. Yet the food they need is hard to find in cold weather, so squirrels bury food to eat during the winter. Because they do not remember where they bury the food, they must find it with their sense of smell. Squirrels can detect pine cones under a foot of dirt. Some of their stored nuts are never found, however, and these grow into trees.

By the time young flying squirrels are two months old, they have ventured out of the nest and have discovered how to glide. But until then, they must be well cared for. During their first two months of life, they depend completely on their mothers for food. Even with their mothers' protection and later with their gliding skill, fewer than one-half of all flying squirrels live as long as one year.

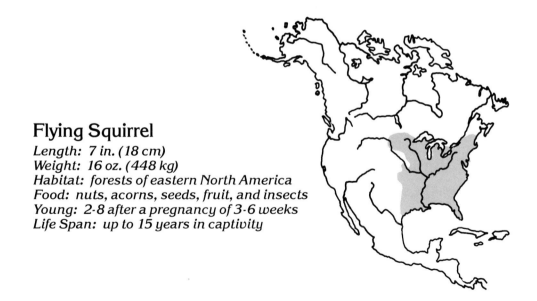

Flying Squirrel
Length: 7 in. (18 cm)
Weight: 16 oz. (448 kg)
Habitat: forests of eastern North America
Food: nuts, acorns, seeds, fruit, and insects
Young: 2-8 after a pregnancy of 3-6 weeks
Life Span: up to 15 years in captivity

PORCUPINE

The name **porcupine** means "quill pig." This animal is not really a pig, however. Like the guinea pig, it is a rodent. But its quills are real and are just as dangerous as they look. Without them, the porcupine would have a tough time surviving.

Unlike most small animals, porcupines are slow and clumsy. Any meat-eater that wants to catch one can do so with no trouble. Yet, thanks to its quills, few meat-eaters will bother a porcupine.

The quills are sharp, tough spines that are mixed in with the soft hairs on the animal's back. They are lined with hooked points like the barbs on fishhooks. This makes it almost impossible for another animal to pull the quills out once they enter its skin. It is not true that porcupines can shoot their quills like arrows. When attacked, the porcupine tucks its head and turns its back to the enemy.

It tries to swat the foe with its tail. When it does, the loose quills stick in the attacker's face.

These painful jabs protect the porcupine from most attackers. But an animal called a **fisher** has found a way to get around this defense. The fisher is a large member of the weasel family. It can move quickly enough to flip the porcupine over without getting hurt. The porcupine's belly has no quills and cannot hurt the fisher as it feeds. Porcupines rarely survive an attack by a fisher.

Although heavy and awkward, North American porcupines are good climbers. Their young can climb trees a few days after they are born. The animals' strong, curved claws help them go high up into evergreen trees. During the winter, they live off evergreen needles and bark. In the summer, porcupines spend more time on the ground eating leaves, buds, and fruit. They rest most of the day and feed at dawn, at dusk, and on moonlit nights.

In areas where there are no fishers, porcupines are often

considered pests and can ruin many trees by stripping the bark. The porcupines' love of salt also causes problems. Attracted by the salt in human sweat, they often chew canoe paddles. In winter, they may chew car tires that are coated with road salt. When porcupines cause too much damage, fishers are sometimes brought in. Defenseless against this enemy, porcupine numbers usually drop quickly.

Porcupine

Length: 29 in. (73 cm)
Weight: 30-40 lb. (14-18 kg)
Habitat: evergreen forests of North America
Food: bark, leaves, stems, buds, and fruit
Young: 1-4 after a pregnancy of 2-7 months
Life Span: up to 20 years in captivity

MARA

The mara looks like a small antelope with a rabbit's head. It lies down with its forelegs out in front, just like a dog. But it is not a rabbit, an antelope, or a dog. The mara is actually a long-legged relative of rodents such as the guinea pig and porcupine.

Maras live on the dry plains of Argentina in South America. Few plants and little water can be found on this windswept ground, but maras are well suited for living there. Thick pads protect their feet from the hard ground, and they get most of the water they need from plants. Like other rodents, they have sharp front teeth that never stop growing. So they constantly wear them down by gnawing on tough grasses and shrubs.

Maras enjoy lying in the warm sunlight. But like the other prey animals in this book, they can rarely relax.

Maras run much faster than a human. They have an unusual way of bouncing along with all four legs off the ground at once. But if they are surprised, they can easily be caught and killed by foxes and other enemies.

The problem of guarding the young is made easier by "nurseries." These are underground homes, or **burrows**, that female maras dig in the ground. The females give birth next to the opening into the burrow. Then the one to three newborns quickly crawl down to safety. Up to 15 females will put their young in one burrow. That way, they can take turns watching the burrow while the others eat.

Maras are born with teeth and are able to eat grass and other plants one day after their birth. Yet the mothers make sure the young are fed. Babies drink milk from their mothers for up to four months. The females will nurse only their own young. Because they spend so much time being mothers, the female mara needs to eat more than the male. The male helps out by standing guard over the female nearly every waking moment. His long ears flick this way and that to catch any warning sounds.

Unlike most mammals, a male and female mara stay together their whole lives. Yet they are rarely seen together. In fact, the female hardly seems to notice the male. But her mate makes sure nothing gets in her way. Even if another male mara comes within 100 feet (30 m) of his partner, a male will drive him away.

Mara

Length: 24-29 in. (60-73 cm)
Weight: 20-35 lb. (9-16 kg)
Habitat: dry grasslands of South America
Food: grasses and other plants
Young: 1-3 after a pregnancy of 3 months
Life Span: up to 10 years in captivity

ARCTIC HARE

Hares and rabbits are some of the most nervous animals in the world. They have good reason to be scared. They are one of the favorite foods of many meat-eaters. Some species of rabbits are hunted by as many as 40 different kinds of animals. Foxes, lynxes, coyotes, eagles, hawks, owls, and wolves are some of the creatures that depend on these animals for food. Living in such a dangerous world, it is no wonder that hares sometimes die of fright when cornered.

Although they cannot fight back, hares are not totally defenseless. Most can outrun the animals that hunt them. They have many kinds of early warning systems that tell them when danger is near. Their long ears can hear very quiet noises. They have large eyes that can see in a full circle. Finally, their noses can pick up smells that warn them of danger.

Most rabbits and hares are also expert hiders. When they lie still, their furry coats blend in with the land around them. The arctic hare is the best example of this. During the summer, arctic hares are greyish brown and blend in well with the ground. When winter comes, their short, brown hair falls off, and longer, warmer, white hair grows in its place. This makes it very hard to find the hare when it lies in the snow. The change of coats is caused by changes in the amount of daylight and by changes in temperature. Because of this, a hare can be well hidden no matter where it lives. Arctic hares living in somewhat warmer parts of the Soviet Union are white for five months in a year. In Ireland, where it is warmer still, the arctic hares never change to white at all. Yet those that live where the snow never melts north of the arctic circle remain white year 'round.

Even with their speed and hiding, hares rarely escape meat-eaters for long. More than 9 out of every 10 hares are killed in their first year of life. The species is in no danger of dying out, however, because hares can produce babies quickly. A female hare is ready to have babies at six months of age and can give birth as many as four times a year. With up to 8 babies, or **leverets**, in a litter, a hare may produce more than 30 babies in one year. Even if most of these are killed, two or three healthy hares keep the population growing.

Arctic Hare

Length: 21 in. (53 cm) including ears
Weight: 9 lb. (4 kg)
Habitat: tundra of Asia, Europe,
and North America
Food: grasses, herbs, and shrubs
Young: 2-8 after a pregnancy
of 6 weeks
Life Span: up to 7 years in captivity

ANTELOPE JACKRABBIT

The antelope jackrabbit's name is full of mistakes. The animal is not a rabbit at all, but a hare. The antelope part of the name comes from the white hairs on its tail that stand up when the animal is scared. This "white flag" warns other jackrabbits of danger. An animal that people thought was an antelope also does this, and so the hare was called an antelope jackrabbit. That antelope, however, was actually a pronghorn. So a better name for this animal would have been a pronghorn hare.

Hares and rabbits are much alike. Both are food for foxes, coyotes, lynxes, eagles, and hawks. But there are some differences. Most rabbits dig burrows, and most hares do not. Instead, hares usually make nests in shallow dips in the ground. Rabbits are more likely to hide from danger while hares are faster and will try to outrun danger. Rabbits are born blind and hairless and must be cared for.

Hares are born with fur, open eyes, and legs that are ready to run. They are sometimes left on their own right after birth. Rabbits stay close to their homes all their lives. Hares are likely to travel farther in search of food. Hares are also larger than rabbits, with longer legs and ears.

Jackrabbits are the largest and fastest of the hares. An adult antelope jackrabbit is about 21 inches (53 cm) long. It has enormous, seven-inch (18-cm) ears. These thin ears are full of blood vessels. The blood is cooled by close contact with the air, which helps the antelope jackrabbit to survive in the heat of the southwestern United States. Jackrabbits keep alert to danger. They turn their ears to catch sounds from every direction and wrinkle and twitch their noses to pick up scents. If they sense danger, they stand perfectly still, hoping they cannot be seen. If an enemy gets too close, they dash off. Jackrabbits can leap more than 10 feet (300 cm). With an ability to run 40 miles (64 km) an hour, they are one of the fastest animals on earth.

The hares' appetite has angered farmers and ranchers for years. Feeding during the night, 30 jackrabbits eat as much as a large sheep. Antelope jackrabbits use their sharp teeth to clip off plants that other animals cannot eat. They will even eat cactus for both food and water. Because they are able to eat so many kinds of plants, hares can be found almost anywhere.

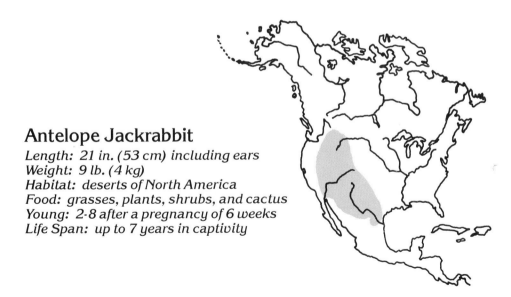

Antelope Jackrabbit

Length: 21 in. (53 cm) including ears
Weight: 9 lb. (4 kg)
Habitat: deserts of North America
Food: grasses, plants, shrubs, and cactus
Young: 2-8 after a pregnancy of 6 weeks
Life Span: up to 7 years in captivity

PIKA

Some prey animals can use their small size to their advantage. The pika, for example, escapes meat-eating animals by going underground. It makes its home in rock piles and narrow spaces in mountain walls. Pikas are usually safe there, because such places are too cramped for larger animals to squeeze into. Although they often sit on rocks out in the open, they can quickly dash to safety.

But the pikas must leave their safe perches to find food. Then they face danger from all directions. Hawks strike from above, and weasels hunt them on the ground.

Although pikas do not like to be seen, they do like to be heard. They help each other by giving a warning when danger approaches. This high-pitched noise sounds like a whistle. Some people call these small members of the rabbit family "whistling hares" because of these sounds.

Pikas also whistle to warn other pikas to stay away from their territory. This whistling can go on day and night. Although large numbers of the animals live in the same area, pikas are not friendly neighbors. Each guards its own territory closely and will chase away any other pika that wanders too near. Pikas will not even share food and space with family members, and young pikas must find their own homes when they are just a few weeks old.

The soft, furry pikas do not hibernate. However, there is little to eat once the mountains are covered with snow. So pikas work hard during the summer and autumn to collect a food supply. They cut down far more green plants, grasses, flowers, and leaves than they can eat. At night, they drag the pile of food under the cover of overhanging rocks. Then in the daytime, they spread it out to dry in the sun. If it rains, pikas pack up their food and haul it to cover. Every day, the pile gets larger, and still the pikas drag their food supply around. By the end of summer, these "haystacks" can be several feet high. The pikas then store it away to eat during the winter. They defend their supplies as fiercely as they defend their territory.

When the winter storms come, pikas may be buried under snow for weeks at a time. But pikas can tunnel easily through the snow, which keeps them hidden from enemies when they leave their secret shelters.

Pika

Length: 6-10 in. (15-25 cm)
Weight: 6-14 oz. (168-392 g)
Habitat: mountains of western North America
Food: grasses, herbs, leaves, and twigs
Young: 2-6 after a pregnancy of 4 weeks
Life Span: up to 3 years in captivity

VICUNA

Most members of the camel family do not need to worry about protection. This group, which also includes llamas, is watched over by human masters. But a kind of llama known as the vicuna runs wild in South America. Only three feet (90 cm) high at the shoulders, this gentle animal appears to be easy prey for foxes, dogs, and mountain lions.

The shy, nervous vicunas are always alert to danger and, like most prey animals, they avoid stronger creatures. When one notices an enemy, it whistles loudly to warn the others. Then they all run off, with the strongest male bringing up the rear.

Even so, the vicunas' greatest protection is their mountain home. Not many dangerous animals can reach the vicunas' feeding grounds on mountain slopes and meadows at least two miles (3 km) above sea level. Only a few mountain lions and occasional dogs or foxes threaten them there.

For added safety, vicunas go even higher up the mountains to sleep. Their surefooted hooves help them climb steep slopes to the very highest ridges.

The treeless mountaintops can be windy and cold. Yet the vicuna stays warm under its coat of fine wool. There were once millions of these animals roaming the mountains of South America until people began killing them for their wool. Only a few thousand vicunas survived. Now they are protected by law from hunters, and their numbers are growing.

Vicunas eat grass, one of the few plants that can grow in such high places. The animals do so much chewing that the grass wears away their teeth. Fortunately, vicunas' teeth never stop growing and whatever is worn away is replaced by new growth.

Vicunas usually live in small families of from 4 to 15 animals. One male takes charge of a group of several females and their young and makes all the decisions for the group. They eat and sleep whenever and wherever he chooses. In return, the male is expected to protect the others. The 100-pound (45-kg) vicunas are not equipped for defense, but the male usually puts himself between the females and danger. When the young males become a year old, the leader chases them out of the group. These young male vicunas then band together in large herds until they are able to control families of their own.

Vicuna

Height: 36 in. (90 cm) at shoulder
Weight: 100 lb. (45 kg)
Habitat: dry areas of the mountains of South America
Food: grasses, herbs, and other plants
Young: 1 after a pregnancy of 11 months
Life Span: up to 28 years in captivity

MALAYAN TAPIR

Tapirs have been around longer than most other mammals and are large, strong animals. The Malayan tapir can grow eight feet (240 cm) long and weigh 700 pounds (315 kg). Yet even with its size, the tapir must always keep a careful watch for enemies. One slip and a tapir becomes an easy meal for a tiger.

Tapirs can be easily mistaken for pigs. They have heavy bodies, short legs, and short trunks that look like pig snouts. They like to wallow in the mud. But they are actually more closely related to the rhinoceros and zebra.

The Malayan tapir lives in the swamps and forests of southeast Asia where plants grow thickly. Tapirs do not like to be standing targets while eating, so they zigzag their way through the brush and eat only a few leaves from each plant. Their squat bodies allow them to shove their way, and even run, through dense thickets.

Because tapirs have poor eyesight, they must rely heavily on their sense of smell. These animals walk with their trunks close to the ground to pick up scents. They can also use their trunks to pull leaves and shoots within reach of their mouths.

Although they are large creatures, tapirs are rarely seen in the wild. They have few defenses against the big meat-eaters, so they must stay hidden. The shy animals even stay away from other tapirs because it is easier for one tapir to hide than for a group. During the day, they sleep while hidden in thickets. When they come out to feed at night, they stay near the water. Tapirs are good divers and swimmers and will dive underwater to avoid tigers and other enemies. Tapirs spend so much time in water that in some parts of the world they are called water pigs.

The Malayan tapir is also sometimes called the saddled tapir. With its white back and black legs, it is easy to see why. This unusual coloring seems as though it would attract attention. But it actually helps the tapir stay hidden. The tapir is most active in the night shadows and moonlight. In such light, its black and white coat makes the animal very difficult to see and gives them an edge that has helped them survive the attacks of the tiger for centuries.

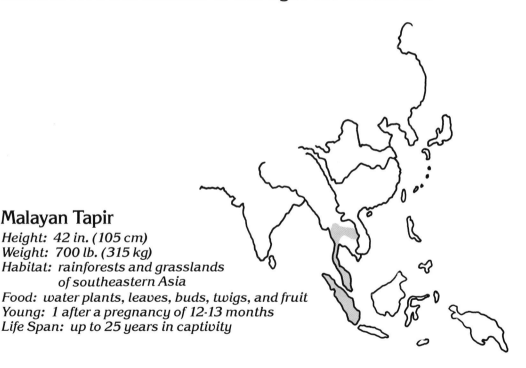

Malayan Tapir
Height: 42 in. (105 cm)
Weight: 700 lb. (315 kg)
Habitat: rainforests and grasslands
of southeastern Asia
Food: water plants, leaves, buds, twigs, and fruit
Young: 1 after a pregnancy of 12-13 months
Life Span: up to 25 years in captivity

ZEBRA

There is no place to hide on the flat African plains. Hungry lions and hyenas have no trouble finding zebras. Fast legs and watchful eyes are the zebras' only hope of staying alive.

Healthy zebras are too large and strong for most meat-eaters to catch, but hyenas sometimes catch sick or old ones. They chase the herd until a weak zebra gets tired and then attack it. Lions, however, will kill any zebra they can get close to. In most cases, zebras will see the lions in time. They can run faster than lions, so when a lion charges, zebras zigzag across the plains. If they can stay away from the lion for the first few seconds of the chase, they are safe, at least until the next attack.

Some people think that the zebras' stripes help them hide from lions. They think that the stripes blend in with the background at night, which is when lions usually hunt. Others do not think the stripes confuse the lions at all.

Their research shows that zebras have stripes because they are attractive. Zebras seem to like stripes. They are more friendly toward zebras that have bold stripes and less friendly to the few that have no stripes. Stripes may help the animals tell each other apart. Like fingerprints, no two sets of zebra stripes are alike.

Even if the stripes help the zebra hide, the animals are rarely quiet or alone. They gather in large, noisy herds of up to 10,000 animals. Although they may wander off in smaller groups, they do not go far from a water hole. Zebras need to drink often and usually come to the water in a group. That way, there are many eyes to watch for danger.

In dry seasons, the zebras scatter into smaller groups. They may roam hundreds of miles as they search for food and water. Their hard hooves help them run over ground that would be too rocky for horses. Zebras also use their hooves to dig for water that is under the ground.

Zebras eat many kinds of tall grasses and often feed on grass that is too tough for other animals to eat. This grass does not have much nutrition, however. Zebras often graze night and day to get all that they need to survive. During the night, they stay on the flattest land, where they can see danger coming. Like all horses, zebras have large, farseeing eyes. They can also twist their ears to listen to sounds all around them.

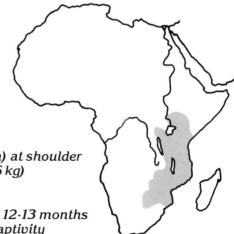

Zebra
Height: 41-59 in. (103-148 cm) at shoulder
Weight: 440-880 lb. (198-396 kg)
Habitat: grasslands of Africa
Food: grasses
Young: 1 after a pregnancy of 12-13 months
Life Span: up to 25 years in captivity

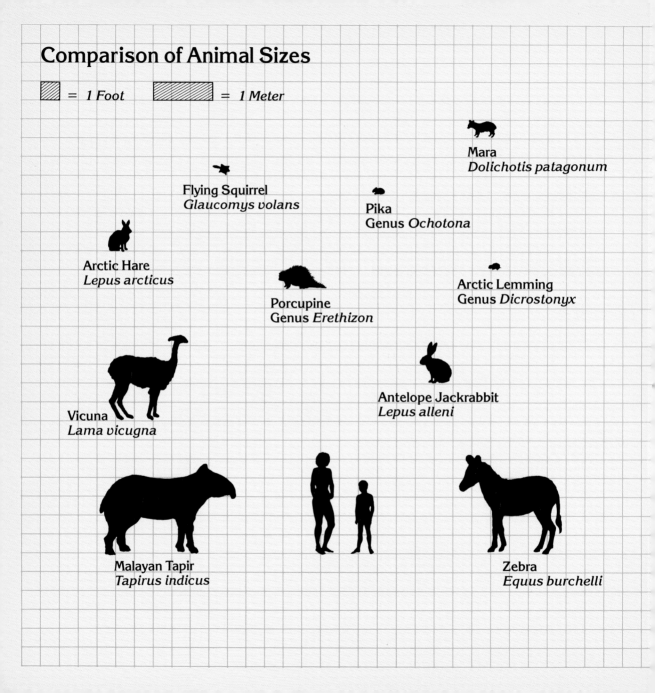

Comparison of Animal Sizes

▨ = 1 Foot   ▨▨▨ = 1 Meter

Mara
Dolichotis patagonum

Flying Squirrel
Glaucomys volans

Pika
Genus *Ochotona*

Arctic Hare
Lepus arcticus

Porcupine
Genus *Erethizon*

Arctic Lemming
Genus *Dicrostonyx*

Vicuna
Lama vicugna

Antelope Jackrabbit
Lepus alleni

Malayan Tapir
Tapirus indicus

Zebra
Equus burchelli